# HOW TO EASILY SELF-PUBLISH A PAPERBACK BOOK

## A Guide For the Not So Savvy

Chad O

ISBN: 9781795723466

This book is dedicated to all those
with a story to tell.

# FOREWORD

*"To live is to live with death all the time."*

Jiddu Krishnamurti

Everyone has a story to tell. Everyone has a book inside them waiting to be written and published and in the past it's been a little different. Writing a book is a huge hurdle in and of itself but back in the day, the second half would prove to be the bigger challenge. That is, getting published but not anymore.

Today, anyone can self-publish a book and it costs nothing. There are no page number requirements, there are no strict guidelines to follow, and there are no gatekeepers. One can publish a book with all kinds of errors with only a few pages. There's no one there to say "This isn't going to cut it" but you.

Also, I understand that self-publishing on the internet for those who want to pull their hair whenever they hear the word 'computer' can be a stumbling block. Computers can be scary for some of us and that's why I've created this book. I've put a lot of screen-shots (pictures) of the entire online publishing process to assist the not so savvy in publishing a paperback book.  This way, it leaves very little room for interpretation. Now all that's left to do is to write your book.

Namaste, As Salam U Alaikum, Shalom, and may peace, love, and happiness be upon you all.

# CHAPTER 1: WRITING YOUR BOOK

Writing a book can be complicated but it doesn't have to be. My suggestion is to keep things simple. If you don't know how many chapters or how many pages each chapter should have, I'd say just stick with 3 chapters. Work on one chapter at a time, and when that chapter is done just move on to the next. Don't worry if your chapter only has one page of content. If it's done, it's done.

If you don't know what to write about, here are some questions to help get you started. For me it's helped to ask the following: What's something that I can share with the world, even if it's already been said, what can I say in my own way, that will ease my tormented soul? What are some things the world needs to hear? What are some things that I need to hear? What are some words I could leave with the people I care about?

To know that you don't have to write for anyone but yourself or those you care about was a big help for me in getting my books published. Now, just write! Write one of these questions as a chapter in your book and start writing. If you aren't big on writing, just get a tape recorder or your smartphone and record your thoughts and then have them transcribed or transcribe it yourself.

# CHAPTER 2: GETTING YOUR BOOK IN DIGITAL FORM

Great!  Your book is done and now you're excited to get it published. The next step is to download a "Manuscript Template." To do this go to:

**https://kdp.amazon.com/en_US/help/topic/ G201834230**

Once the template is downloaded you'll want to copy-paste what you've typed (or transcribed) into the template of your choice (click on "Templates With Sample Content" to expand the link and to download your template).  I recommend using the 5"x8" or 6"x9".

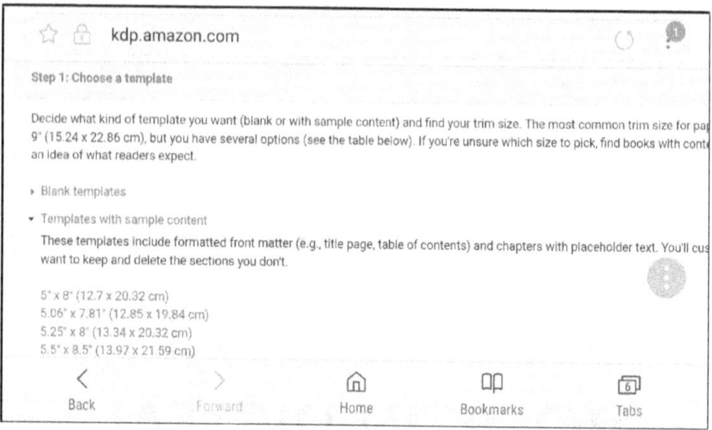



Now that you have a "Manuscript Template" you are going to need a program to open and work with that template. If you have Microsoft Office with Microsoft Word then you're all set. If you don't have Microsoft Word then you can download Libre-Office, which is a free, open-source program that's just like Microsoft Office and it's completely free! I've used this program and it's worked great for me, which may not be the case for you. So please only download and use this program at your own risk.

Link To Download LibreOffice

**https://www.libreoffice.org/download/download/**

Open the "Manuscript Template" that you've downloaded, then fill in the title of your book, author name, dedication page, and copyright info. Fill these portions in manually, meaning without copy and pasting because copy-pasting these portions may overwrite the formatting of the entire template.

Then, delete the rest of the sample content along with the table of contents (I'll show you how to add the table of contents later using Kindle Create which is a lot easier) and then copy-paste the rest of your book. That is your foreword, or introduction page (if you have either), as well as all the chapters of your book.

So by now you should have all of your books content in your template manuscript. You will see that there are page numbers (pagination), as well as the title of your book and your name (or the name of the author) at the top of each page.

If you have any additional questions or for more insights please watch the video here:

**https://kdp.amazon.com/en_US/help/topic/ G201834230**

## Download and Install The "Kindle Create" Program

Here's The Download Link **https://kdp.amazon.com/ en_US/help/topic/GHU4YEWXQGNLU94T**

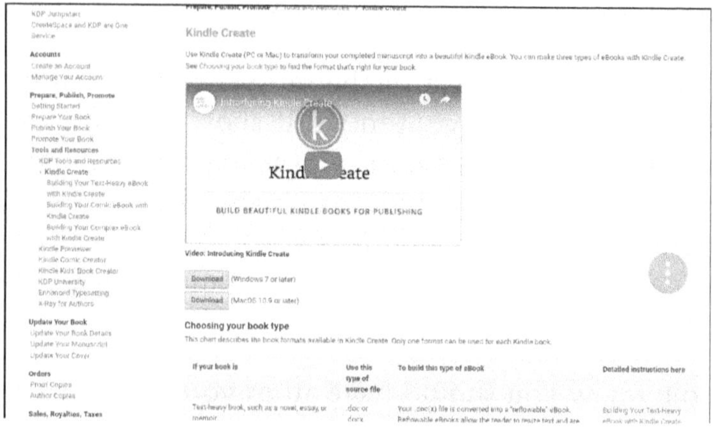

## Import Your Manuscript Template in Kindle Create

Now, open the Kindle Create program, click "New Project From File," then choose "Novels, Essays, Poetry, Narrative Non-fiction" as the type of book and then click the "Choose file" button. Locate your manuscript file (the manuscript template file with the contents of your book) and then select and load it.

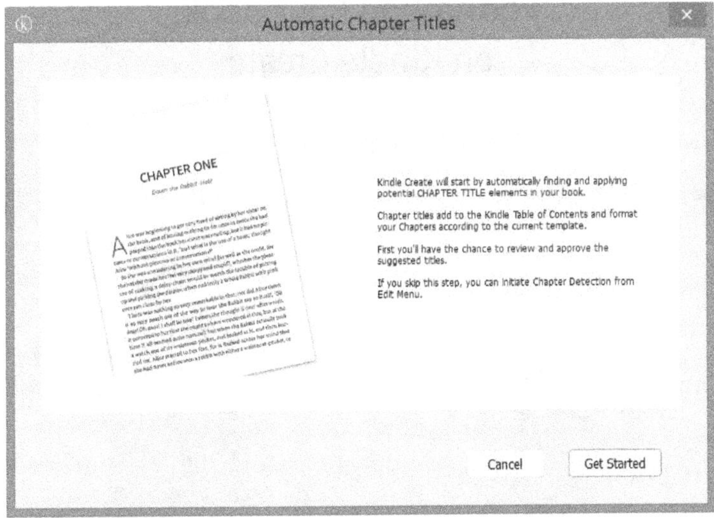

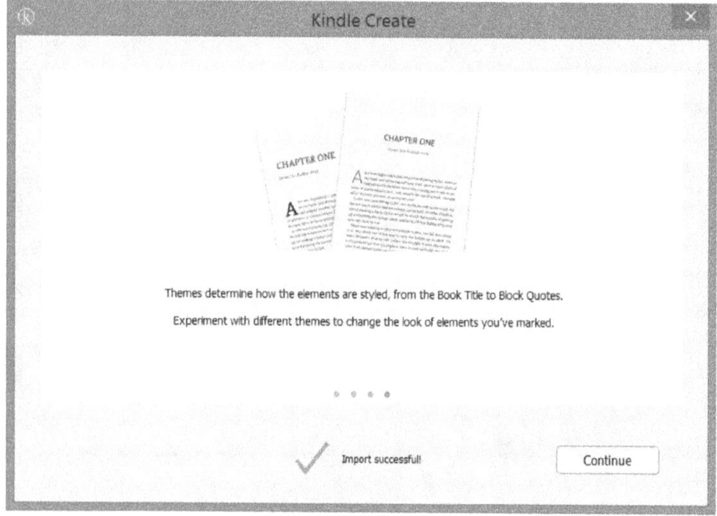

# Formatting Your Book
# on Kindle Create

## Click "Accept Selected"

# Highlight The Title of Your Book and Then Choose "Book Title" As the Element Type.

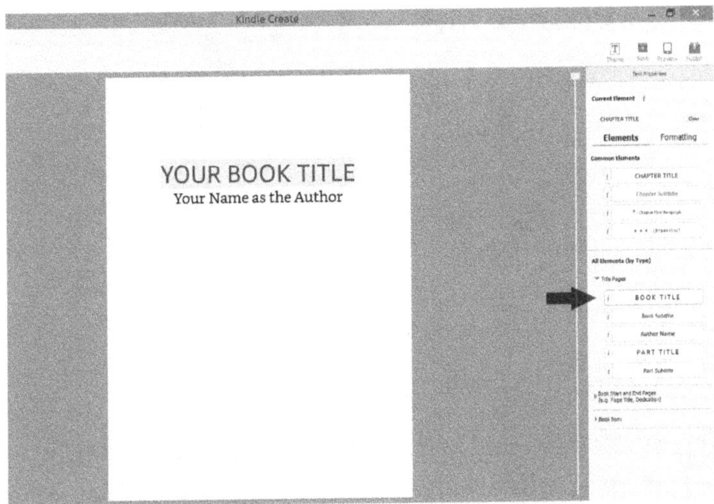


# Highlight The Name of the Author and Choose "Author Name" as the Element Type

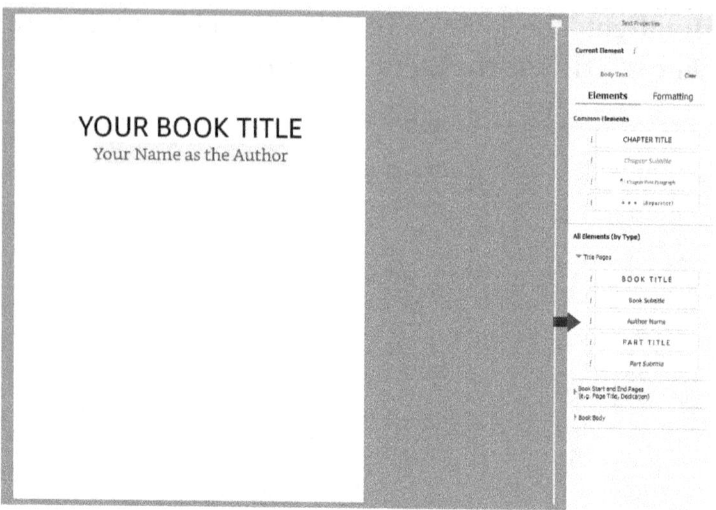

If You Have a Dedication Page Define The Element Type as "Dedication Page" under "Book Start and End Pages."

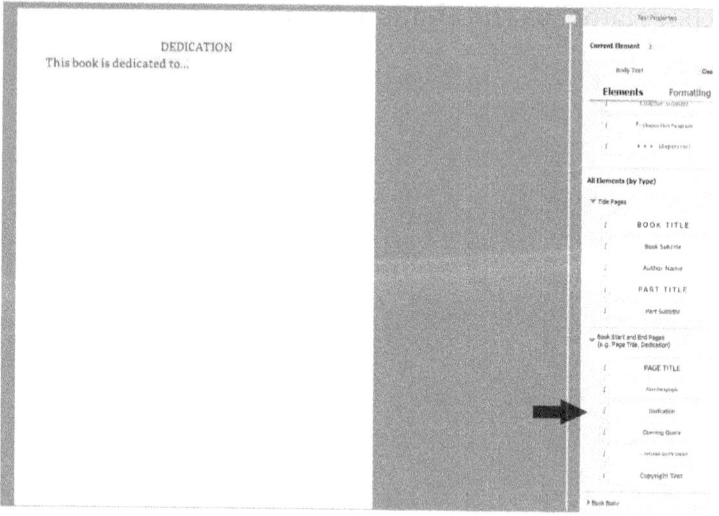

If You Have a Copyright Page Define The Element

Type as "Copyright Text" also under "Book Start and End Pages."

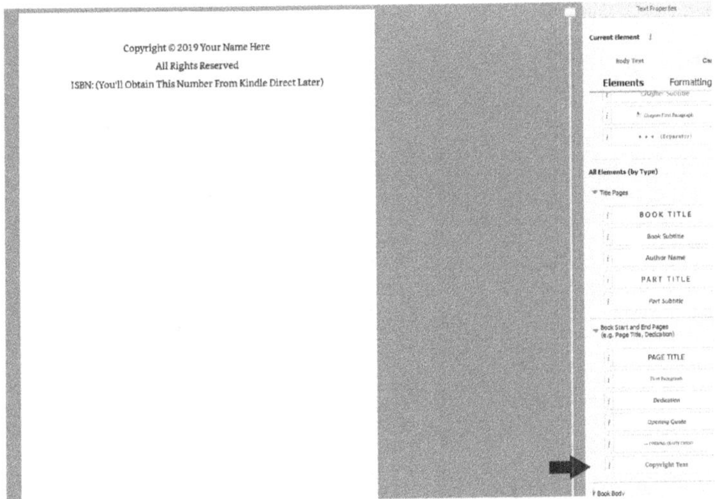

Now, define the chapters in your book there should the "Chapter Title" element button just below "Common Elements." If it's not there then click and expand the arrow at the very bottom next to "Book Body." Do this for every chapter of your book.

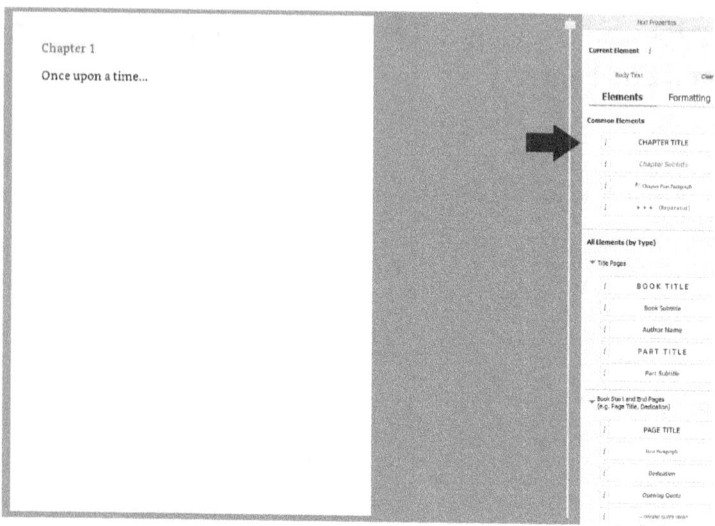

# The Table of Contents

To add the table of contents, simply right-click on the page that comes after (preceding, in front of) where you would like it to appear. That is, the table of contents will appear behind the page that is selected on the right-click.

Check/Uncheck the "Include in Table of Contents" box on the right pane menu to include or exclude any pages or chapters from showing up on the table of contents (This box will show up when a page is selected on the left-pane...).

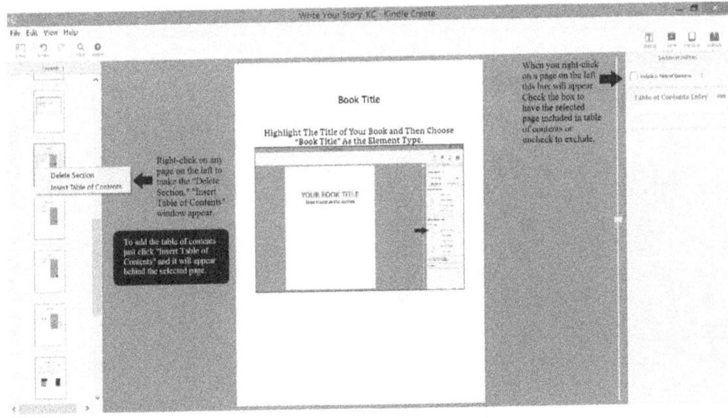

# Check and Re-check The Formatting of Your Book

Once, everything looks good "Save" and "Publish." Take note of where you save this "KPF" file because this is the file that you'll use to upload your manuscript to the Kindle Direct Publishing site.

# Chad O

Kindle Create
File Edit View Help
New Project    Ctrl+N
Open Project    Ctrl+O
Open Recent
Close Project    Ctrl+W
Save Project    Ctrl+S
Save Project As    Ctrl+Shift+S
Publish    Ctrl+Shift+P
Exit
DEDICATION
This book is dedicated to...

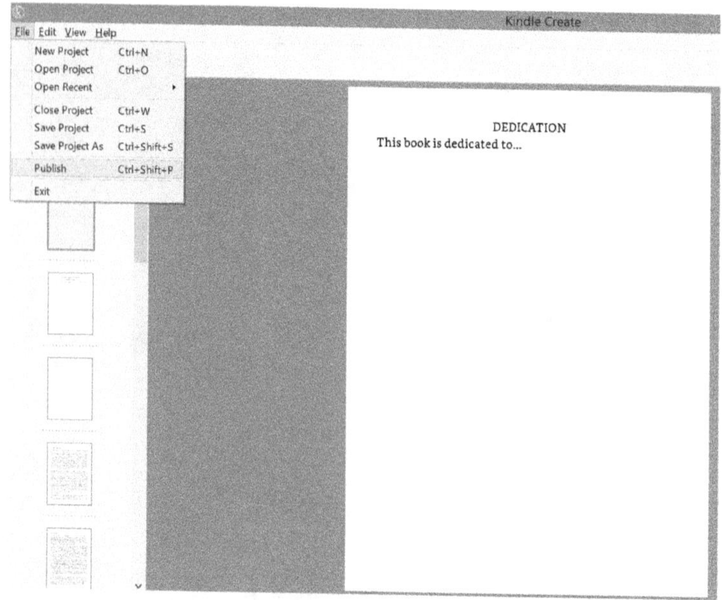

# CHAPTER 3: PUBLISHING YOUR BOOK ON KINDLE DIRECT PUBLISHING

## Uploading Your Book on KDP

To setup a Kindle Direct Publishing account and to be paid for your book, you'll need your social security number (for tax purposes), and a checking account routing and account number.

Create Your Account By Going To **https:// kdp.amazon.com/en_US/**

## Setting Up Your Account

If you are not in the United States please go to the KDP page that's specific to your region.

Once your account has been setup, begin to setup a paperback copy of your book by clicking the "+ Paperback" link.

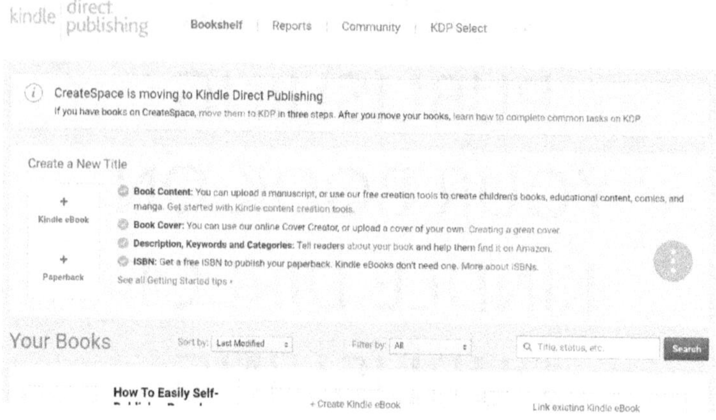

On the next page ("Paperback Details"), to keep things simple only enter the information on the following fields: Book Title, Primary Author or Contributor (This will most likely be your first and last name), Description, check the box "I own the copyright and I hold necessary publishing rights," enter any related keywords (I usually type words that are related or relevant to the content of my book), choose two categories in the categories section, under "Adult Content" check the appropriate box, and then save and continue.

On the following page click "Assign me a free KDP ISBN" unless you have your own ISBN number in which case you'll check the "Use my own ISBN" box and enter the number there.

Leave the publication date field blank and the date when your book actually goes live will be used automatically.

## Print Options

Leave all the fields as they are. The only thing that I've changed was the trim size. I've changed the 6"x9" to 5"x8". Choose the size "Manuscript Template" that you've downloaded and used.

# Upload Your Manuscript

Click on the "Upload paperback manuscript" button and then locate your "KPF" file and then upload it.

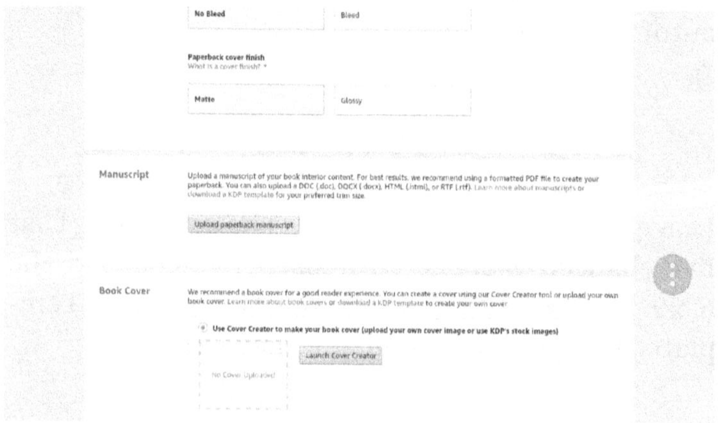

## Create a Cover For Your Book

To get started click "Launch Cover Creator."

Once you've launched the cover creator, just click the "X" or "Continue" to get out of the "How to Use Cover Creator" screen.

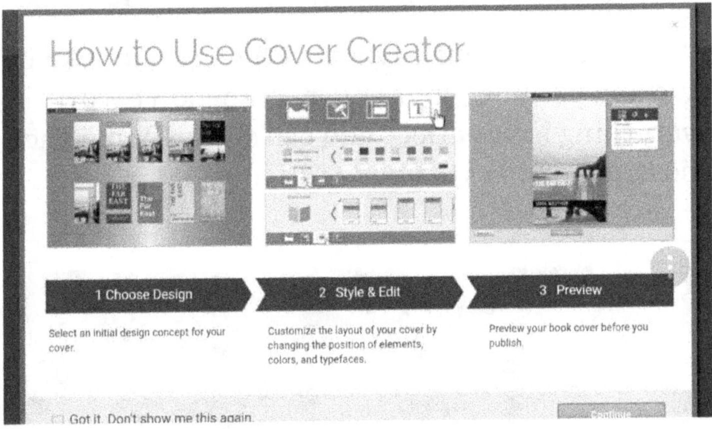


Now, choose an image from the image gallery. If you have your own image then choose "From My Computer." If you don't have an image then you can choose an image by clicking "From Image Gallery." If you don't want to use an image then "Skip This Step."

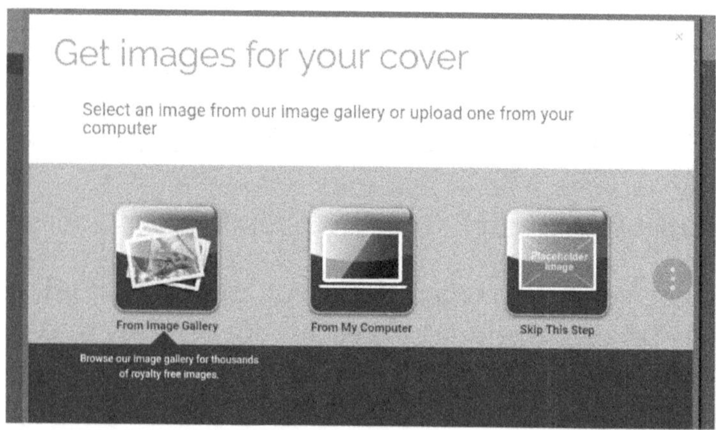

Once you have your cover exactly how you like it, save and preview your cover.  Also, don't worry if everything isn't perfect you can always come back and make changes to your book cover later.

Now, click "Launch Previewer" to preview your book. Check to ensure that your book looks the way you want, and that all your pages and chapters are in there.  If everything looks good then close the preview and go to the next page.

## Rights and Pricing

This section is self-explanatory. Read through each section and then choose a price for your book. Then go all the way to the bottom and publish your book. It will usually take a few days for your book to be reviewed and to be live.

Also, keep in mind that you can make changes to the content of your book, the cover of your book, as well as description and keywords, and pricing. So don't fret if everything isn't absolutely perfect. The things you can't change are the title (and/or subtitle), the bleed settings, trim size, and interior & paper type.

At this point you'll probably want to go and celebrate but just hold on before you do. Now, that you're done with your paperback copy you'll want to go and publish a Kindle copy.

## Publishing A Kindle Copy

This is going to be a breeze. To get started just click "+ Kindle ebook" under create a new title.

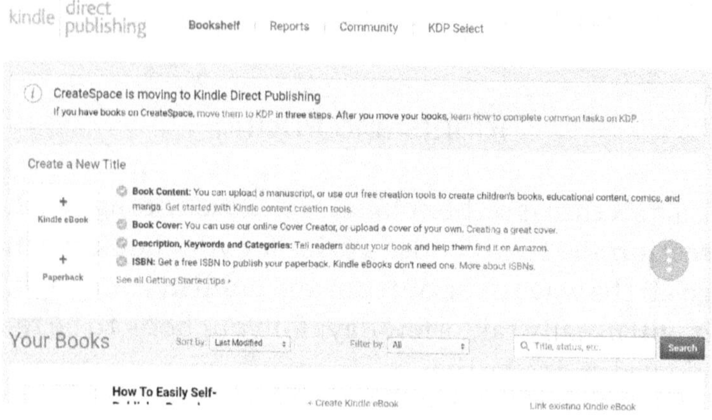

All the steps are exactly the same as the paper copy except you'll find that it's a lot easier because a lot of the fields are prepopulated with the information from your paperback copy.

# Congratulations! You're a Just a Few Days Away From Being a Published Author

By now, you have both a paperback copy and a Kindle copy of your book being reviewed and you're probably pretty excited because soon you can actually say that you're a published author. Congratulations! Give yourself a big pat on the back.

# WEBSITE

https://www.mag.dipitum.com

Notes:

Chad O

Notes:

Notes:

Chad O

Notes:

Notes:

Chad O

Notes:

Notes:

Chad O

Notes:

Notes:

www.ingramcontent.com/pod-product-compliance
Lightning Source LLC
Chambersburg PA
CBHW050803240726
48654CB00008B/609